One Nose, Two Hands

Una nariz, dos manos

Un nez, deux mains

一鼻，兩手

text by Jocelyn Graeme photos by May Henderson

Addison-Wesley Publishers Limited
Don Mills, Ontario • Reading, Massachusetts
Menlo Park, California • New York
Wokingham, England • Amsterdam • Bonn
Sydney • Singapore • Tokyo • Madrid • San Juan

One nose smelling.

Un nez qui sent.

Una nariz olfateando.

一鼻聞。

Two hands holding.

Deux mains qui se tiennent.

Dos manos tomándose.

兩手牽。

Three mouths smiling.

Trois bouches qui sourient.

Tres bocas sonriendo.

三口笑。

Four feet hopping.

Quatre pieds qui sautillent.

Cuatro pies brincando.

四脚跳。

Five fingers drumming.

Cinq doigts qui tambourinent.

Cinco dedos tamborileando.

五指鼓。

Six eyes peeking.

Six yeux qui regardent.

Seis ojos mirando.

六眼窺。

Seven heads thinking.

Sept têtes qui pensent.

Siete cabezas pensando.

七頭想。

Eight arms reaching.

Huit bras qui s'étendent.

Ocho brazos alcanzando.

八手伸。

Nine stomachs rumbling.

Neuf ventres qui gargouillent.

Nueve estómagos retumbando.

九肚響。

Ten friends sharing.

Dix amis qui partagent.

Diez amigos compartiendo.

十友分。

one	six
two	seven
three	eight
four	nine
five	ten

un	six
deux	sept
trois	huit
quatre	neuf
cinq	dix

uno	seis
dos	siete
tres	ocho
cuatro	nueve
cinco	diez

一
兩
三
四
五

六
七
八
九
十

Sponsoring Editor: Beth Bruder

Designer: Pamela Kinney

Editor: Lauren E. Wolk

Translators
Spanish: Edith Stagni
Brenda Cortes

French: Katherine Stauble
Martine Brassard

Chinese: Mei-lin Cheung
Sew Pim Lim
Hsiao Chiang

Sponsor: Early Childhood Multicultural Services
Early Childhood Multicultural Services gratefully acknowledges the support and financial assistance of the Multiculturalism Directorate, Secretary of State, Canada; the Cabinet Committee on Cultural Heritage, Province of British Columbia; and the Preschool ESL Committee (PRESL), Vancouver.

Canadian Cataloguing in Publication Data

Graeme, Jocelyn, 1958–
One nose, two hands

(Hand in hand)
Text in English, Chinese, French, Spanish.
ISBN 0-201-54650-7 (set). – ISBN 0-201-54659-0. (School Edition)
ISBN 0-201-54741-4 (Trade Edition)

1. Body, Human – Juvenile literature. 2. Counting
– Juvenile literature.   I. Henderson, May.
II. Title.   III. Series: Hand in hand (Don Mills,
Ont.).

QP37.G73 1990   612   C90-094223-1

ISBN 0-201-54659-0 (School Edition)   **ISBN 0-201-54741-4** (Trade Edition)

Printed in Canada

A B C D E F – ALG – 95 94 93 92 91 90